The Self-Esteem *Guided Journal*

A 10-WEEK PROGRAM

MATTHEW M^cKAY, PH.D.

CATHARINE SUTKER

New Harbinger Publications, Inc.

Publisher's Note

Distributed in Canada by Raincoast Books.

Copyright © 2005 by Matthew McKay and Catharine Sutker
New Harbinger Publications, Inc.
5674 Shattuck Avenue
Oakland, CA 94609
www.newharbinger.com

Cover design by Amy Shoup
Acquired by Tesilya Hanauer
Edited by Carole Honeychurch

Library of Congress Cataloging in Publication Data on file
ISBN 1-57224-402-X Paperback

Printed in the United States of America

Library of Congress Cataloging-in-Publication Data

McKay, Matthew.
  The self-esteem guided journal : a 10-week program / Matthew McKay and Catharine Sutker.
     p. cm.
  ISBN 1-57224-402-X
  1. Self-esteem. 2. Diaries—Authorship. I. Sutker, Catharine. II. Title.
  BF697.5.S46M35 2005
  158.1—dc22
                                        2005018923
07 06 05

10 9 8 7 6 5 4 3 2 1

First printing

To the memory of Peter D. Rogers. I miss you, my friend.
—MM

To Granny
—CS

Contents

Introduction: The Nature of Self-Esteem

Self-esteem is composed of two things: a belief and a feeling. The belief is a judgment about your overall worth, a summary evaluation of your traits, habits, and abilities. The feeling is a core sense of being good or bad. At its worst, the feeling can be so painful, so acid-etched, that it can make you run away from many of life's challenges. Things like finding a partner, building a career, or developing a support system of friends become so much harder when you feel like a bad or unworthy person.

How Self-Esteem Gets Damaged

While the habit of judgment comes from a basic survival mechanism—needing to sort the world into what's dangerous or desirable—the decision that we are unworthy comes from one of two things. The first is what are called negative *identity messages*. These are the thoughtless, negative judgments we endure growing up. Parents, peers, and teachers all make them: "That's stupid"; "Why can't you do anything right?"; "You ruined it"; "Nice hands, gimp"; "You're plain lazy." Many children hear a lot of this.

Individually, these messages are like drops of water. They roll off of us easily, and they're soon forgotten. But hundreds or thousands of these messages become a river that carves our identity. And it's not just the messages themselves—it's the force or anger behind them that also does damage. When a father shouts, "You screw everything up," the cutting power of the message comes as much from his rage as his words, eroding his child's positive sense of self.

The second way our self-esteem gets damaged is by trauma—things that happened when we were growing up where we felt truly in danger. Physical and sexual abuse, for example, leave a deep impact on self-esteem. That's because the fear associated with trauma makes whatever we hear, learn, or believe from the event so much more powerful.

Not all trauma comes from direct injury. Many children are wounded by loss and abandonment. A parent who dies or leaves or an illness that renders a family member dysfunctional can make children feel unimportant or somehow to blame.

Whether your self-esteem has been injured by trauma or a string of negative identity messages, the results are the same—a belief that you are flawed and a painful feeling of unworthiness. The solution, also, is the same. You will need to rediscover your intrinsic value.

Rebuilding Healthy Self-Esteem

The Dutch master Breughel was famous for painting a bucolic foreground with strange, sinister objects at the edge of the background of the painting. "Icarus" is an example: Farmers are shown working in pastoral fields while a tiny Icarus falls to his death in the background sky. Our own self-portrait often resembles a Breughel painting—there's much that's good and attractive, with some painful, disturbing things around the edges.

Because of the habit of judgment, admixed with trauma or old identity messages, we tend to pay attention to what's painful in our self-portrait, overlooking what's good or affirming. We are watching Icarus fall instead of the lovely fields or the farmers at their work.

Rebuilding self-esteem starts with paying attention to what's good in your self-portrait. It requires a deliberate redirection of focus away from what's wrong with you and toward what's right. It requires a shift from old, habitual judgments to a new awareness of your assets and strengths.

A Commitment to Journaling

There is no better way to change what you look at—in the world and in yourself—than with guided journaling. Your journal is a place where you can notice and record new things about your thoughts, feelings, history, and behavior. And where you can finally see, with noonday clarity, the truth about who you are.

For so long the real you—the good and worthy you—has been hidden by the wounds of a thousand hurtful messages. Guided journaling can and will change your self-esteem because it will redefine the qualities in yourself that you value, and reframe the memories that give you identity.

There is hard work to be done in this journal. But it is good work—important work. And though there may be times when you're tempted to give up, we urge you to see the process through. Commit yourself, right now, to the full ten-week program. Because in the end, this journal will be a treasure of new insight and awareness. And it will be the crucible in which a new sense of yourself is forged.

Journals Work

For years, self-help books have encouraged writing with worksheets, fill-in exercises, and self-assessment tools. With this guided journal, you'll work on your self-esteem using writing as a therapeutic tool.

Writing is a powerful tool that has been shown to produce profound changes, both emotionally and physically. Journaling offers a way to better understand and learn from your emotions, feelings, and thoughts. The process of putting words to paper elicits truths you may not even realize you possess. Writing gives you a certain distance and perspective, allowing you to better understand yourself. The ingrained patterns of self-perception become clear and visible on paper.

Over and over again, research points to the fact that writing about thoughts and feelings promotes healing. Through researching expressive writing for his book, *Opening Up: The Healing Power of Expressing Emotions* (1997), James Pennebaker found that writing about your experiences improves physical and mental health. In his study on expressive writing and trauma, Pennebaker found that over 70 percent of the participants reported "that writing helped them to understand both the (traumatic) event and themselves better." Beth Jacobs, Ph.D., author of *Writing for Emotional Balance* (2005), writes that "Each time you write descriptions of positive feelings, you counteract the idea that bad feelings are all you ever experience. Writing about your good experiences reinforces them."

In this ten-week guided journal, you'll have the daily experience of paying attention to the good in yourself. Each day, you'll learn how to notice positive qualities about yourself, begin taking in the positive feedback others offer, and take note of evidence that points to your strengths and abilities. You'll develop a broader picture of yourself that includes a more accurate and healthy self-perception. You'll learn to avoid judging yourself so harshly. Guided journaling is a tool you can use for the rest of your life. Once you complete the ten weeks, you'll know how to use writing as a way to record all of the unique, special, and positive qualities that you possess.

How This Journal Works

This ten-week program begins with a week practicing and journaling about nonjudgment—regarding everything from people in the news to your own behavior. Weeks two and three will focus on discovering your strengths and redefining weaknesses. Weeks four and five will review your past and how it affects your self-esteem.

During week six we will clarify your deepest values and explore the ways you act on them. Week seven focuses on the impact of your thoughts. The Buddha said: "Nothing does more damage than our own unwise thoughts." You will learn and practice six specific ways to change judgments that destroy self-esteem. Week eight will focus on how to hold to your truth and stand up for yourself. In week nine you will explore and journal about experiences with your self-esteem Achilles heel. Week ten will create daily opportunities to experience your worth and will be a launching pad for your future journal activities.

You're on your way to developing an accurate picture of yourself. For perhaps the first time in your life, you will learn to see all of the positive qualities you possess.

Giving Up Judgment

As a species, the habit of judgment is pretty much hardwired into us. We tend to see the objects in our world as good, bad, or irrelevant. Judging a thing "good" means it is pleasurable, desirable, something to seek. Judging a thing "bad" means it is painful, dangerous, something to avoid or reject. Judgment allows humans to determine what helps versus hurts, to make decisions about what to include and exclude from our lives.

So far so good. But the compulsion to judge extends even to ourselves: We make ourselves objects and assign a value of good or bad. And that's where the incredible pain starts—that moment when you experience yourself as bad or unworthy. Because what you're really doing is rejecting and abandoning yourself. You are casting yourself out, along with all the other bad objects of the world. Few human experiences are worse.

While the habit of judgment is built in to our inherited survival strategies, people with injured self-esteem all do something that makes it worse. They judge themselves in order to become good or perfect. They attack themselves as stupid, selfish, or screwed up in a vain attempt to punish bad behavior and get rid of it.

Baseball Hall of Famer Ty Cobb once described the incredible abuse he heaped on himself every time he made a mistake in the field.

He told himself he was incompetent, or he was an embarrassment to the game if he failed a bunt attempt or missed a hard grounder. Amazingly, Cobb attributed some of his greatness to these compulsive self-attacks.

Lots of folks do the same thing. They try to beat themselves into being better people. The self-attacks grow from a hope that someday they won't despise themselves, won't repeat the same stupid mistakes.

Think of your own experience. Suppose you miss a deadline or do a job that has errors. The impulse to kick yourself around is probably huge and stems from the hope that the attack will somehow make you different, make you a person who no longer feels this worthlessness.

Using judgment as a tool to perfect ourselves is addictive—and poisonous. The truth is that compulsive self-judgment doesn't help anyone to be better. All it does is kill your self-esteem.

You might wonder if judgment ever serves a healthy purpose? There is a difference between healthy and unhealthy judgment. A healthy judgment is when you notice that something *feels* good or bad; unhealthy judgment is when you decide it *is* good or bad. Healthy judgment observes your felt experience; unhealthy judgment assigns it a moral weight.

Escaping the habit of unhealthy judgment is going to take practice and discipline. This week you will learn to observe events as a witness, without evaluating or labeling them. You will watch and feel—but not crush your experience under a weight of "badness."

• • • • • • DAY ONE • • • • • •
Nonjudgment with the Media

Today's exploration of nonjudgment will focus on the newspaper and television. When you read the paper or watch the news today, challenge yourself to experience these media without judgment. Read the article about a murder trial or the latest political shenanigans in Washington without any evaluation—good or bad. Absorb the information, but don't attach a judgment to anything. While watching news commentators, listening to sound bites, or observing the lifestyles of the rich and famous, remind yourself that everyone is doing his or her best to survive. Accept that what you read or see or hear reflects an attempt to cope with the challenges of life. Stay neutral; stay detached. Observe but do not judge.

After you've tried this exercise, journal about your experience. What was it like to observe people and events without evaluating them? What did you have to do inside yourself to resist the habit of judgment? How difficult was it to shift your focus from evaluation to mere observation?

• • • • • • DAY TWO • • • • • •
Nonjudgment with Strangers

Today your task is to observe without judgment people on the street, in their cars, passing you in hallways. No matter how they behave, drive, or look, the task today is to experience strangers you encounter without assumptions, interpretations, or good/bad evaluations.

Tonight or throughout your day write in your journal what this felt like. How hard or easy was it to observe the people around you without judging their behavior? What did you find easiest to accept? What did you find hardest?

• • • • • •DAY THREE• • • • • • •
Nonjudgment with Friends and Coworkers

Today we're asking you to explore the experience of acceptance with the people you play and work with. No matter how annoying, stupid, or wrong someone is, see if you can experience their behavior without any evaluation. You notice and observe, but you make no judgments about whether their actions are good or bad. Record in your journal what happens with this experiment. Were you able to resist judgments when they welled up in you? Or was the drive to label and judge too strong? Did you forget your experiment and slide back into your old, habitual patterns?

• • • • • • DAY FOUR • • • • • • •
Nonjudgment with Children

Today's experiment will focus on resisting the impulse to judge kids. If you have your own children, devote the day to experiencing them without evaluation. Whatever they do, resist the idea that it's good or bad. Simply label it as normal, understandable behavior. Children who are not your own can be incredibly annoying. Whatever their behavior—loud, demanding, emotionally intense—try to accept it as a strategy to cope. Experience each child as trying their best to manage in a difficult world. Use your journal to explore everything you learn from this exercise.

• • • • • • DAY FIVE • • • • • •
Nonjudgment with Parents and Relatives

Today we're asking you to focus your efforts on parents and other rela-
tives. Think about and visualize your parents, aunts, uncles, siblings, and
other members of your family. Try to hold an image of each person in
your mind. As you focus on each family member, be aware of their traits,
tendencies, and anything significant you know about their history. Now
make a real effort to see that person without judgment, without any
thoughts of good or bad. Explore in your journal how this exercise feels
and what it's like attempting to shift your focus from judgment to
acceptance.

• • • • • • DAY SIX • • • • • • •
Nonjudgment with Your Partner
(Past or Present)

Today's exercise involves trying to see your partner with clear eyes. Instead of using the lens that separates everything they do into categories of good or bad, really make an effort to accept them as they are. Watch or visualize your partner, and say to yourself, "They're doing the best they can."

How difficult is it for you to detach judgment from your partner? What happens to you emotionally when you observe your partner's behavior through a lens of acceptance? If you've had great difficulty giving up judgments, how do you feel about that? Is that something you want to change?

• • • • • • DAY SEVEN • • • • • • •
Nonjudgment with Yourself

Now comes perhaps the hardest exercise this week. Your task today is to observe yourself without evaluation. Notice how often you slip into judgments about your behavior, your feelings, experiences from the past, and so on. What happens if you try to push these judgments away? How does it feel to observe yourself without labels or a picture of yourself as right or wrong? If you found it difficult or impossible to let go of self-evaluations, how does that feel? What do you want to do about that?

Your Psychological Self-Portrait: The Strengths

We all carry an inner picture of ourselves, a psychological portrait that includes our traits and tendencies, our weaknesses and strengths. Thousands of experiences, conversations, successes, and struggles have colored this portrait. Yet for all the life experience that goes into it, many of us carry a portrait of ourselves that's terribly distorted, that more resembles a fun house mirror than who we really are.

How does this happen? One defining negative memory can sometimes obscure a hundred positive ones. A single hurtful relationship—where you are judged and criticized—can often make you overlook a dozen times when you succeeded and were praised. Consider how the color of vermilion changes a painting. That red is so intense, such a focus for attention, that your eye is drawn there first and always. Negative memories have that effect. They seem to draw our attention in a way that makes it difficult to see anything else. They can define us so that our positive qualities seem to pale or disappear. We end up victims of something called *confirmatory bias*. Once we've formed a distorted, negative view of ourselves, we only pay attention to experiences that seem to confirm or prove that view. We only remember what fits that picture. And so our self-portrait gets more painful, more ugly.

There is a way to change your inner picture, to reverse the damage of confirmatory bias. It will take two weeks of careful journaling, but at the end, your self-portrait will look very different. This week you'll identify your positive qualities in each of six life domains—physical appearance, relating to others, how others see you, how you do on the job (or school), your performance of daily tasks, and mental functioning. Today we'll begin with physical appearance. Tomorrow you'll explore the ways you relate to others. And you'll continue for five more days until you've fully examined your positive traits in each domain.

This is going to be hard. It's a lot easier to list your faults than to recognize your strengths. People frequently have difficulty remembering—or even recognizing—positive qualities. It seems like bragging, which we're discouraged from doing in our culture. And some of our negative qualities, as described earlier, seem to block all awareness of the positives. But we promise, if you stick with this journaling exercise, your image of yourself will start to change.

Physical Appearance

This is often the most difficult thing to look at, but confronting it head-on could pay huge dividends for your self-esteem. There are usually several physical features that we just don't like. And they often seem so glaring that they may obscure the physical traits we do like. What we're about to ask you to do is a head-to-toe inventory of your physical appearance. Think about your hair, eyes, nose, mouth, chin, complexion, skin quality. Then move on to mentally imagining your neck, shoulders, arms, hands, fingers, as well as your chest, abdomen, hips, pubic area, legs, and feet. Visualize the shape or musculature of each of these areas.

Now begin writing a brief description of each part of your body that you like—even a little bit. It may be hard work, but we'll use it to help you later on. Underline the main term (eyes, lips, fingers, etc.) so you can easily review it later, and put down what you like about it. If you want to include particular memories of times you enjoyed or were complimented for that part, you can include those too.

• • • • • • DAY TWO • • • • • •
Relating to Others

Today you will explore the interpersonal domain—all the ways you deal with people. This is a critical area for self-esteem, and we're going to encourage you to examine it thoroughly. Think about the positive ways you express feelings and needs; work collaboratively to solve problems; and show love, support, or interest in others. Also examine the positive ways you relate sexually. As you explore how you relate, think about different people in your life—family, friends, work colleagues. Look for an interpersonal strength with each person you know.

Now begin writing. It often helps to label and underline your interpersonal strengths (warm, open, accepting, etc.) and describe a typical experience that exemplifies it.

• • • • • • DAY THREE • • • • • •
How Others See You

In today's journaling experience, we want you to think of feedback you've gotten about your strengths and personal assets. It might be in the form of compliments, thank-you notes, or some heartfelt appreciation. Again, think of all the people you've known in the past and present. What did they like or value about you? How did they let you know how they felt?

As you begin writing, underline the term or label you use to describe a strength so you can easily review it later. Also write a brief description of how you were told about this particular asset.

• • • • • • DAY FOUR • • • • • •
How You Do on the Job (or at School)

Today is an opportunity to think about how you handle the major tasks at work or school. What do you do well? What parts of your work or school performance have been appreciated by others? Examine each component of your current job. What are the individual skills that you need to succeed (for instance, you're a fast reader, good consensus builder, or good at diagnosing problems)? Think back to past jobs or school environments, and try to remember your successes, as well as particular skills that helped you be effective.

Now, when you're ready, start writing. As you've done on previous days, label and underline each strength so you can review it easily. And perhaps describe a particular time or situation where that strength was especially in evidence.

DAY FIVE
Your Performance of Daily Tasks

Today the focus should be on your strengths in taking care of the daily tasks of life. These include health maintenance, hygiene, creating a pleasing living environment, money management, food preparation, caring for children, and the many things you do to manage your personal and family needs. Give some thought to how you take care of each of these areas, particularly the things you do well.

Now it's time to describe each of these abilities here. Be sure to label and underline each strength so you can find it later. If there are specific examples you're proud of—financial management, home creation, protecting your health, etc.—you might also want to include those here.

DAY SIX
Mental Functioning

The last domain to explore this week is how you use your mind. This includes your reasoning and problem-solving abilities, as well as your capacity for learning new things. Also important here is creativity—not just in the artistic sense, but creative responses to problems and challenges in every arena of life. Consider, too, your areas of special knowledge, wisdom, and insight. What kind of lessons have you learned over the years that have helped you and others?

As you journal, label and underline each of your abilities so you can easily review them later. And give examples, if you wish, of ways these strengths manifest themselves.

• • • • • • DAY SEVEN • • • • • •
Putting It All Together

On this day you're going to do the most important journal work you've attempted so far. It's now time to synthesize and consolidate what you've learned about your personal assets. What makes this so vital is that concept we talked about at the beginning of the week—confirmatory bias. Much of your life you've paid attention to negative events, things you said wrong or did wrong. Things you hoped for and tried that didn't work out. Once you formed a negative view of yourself, your focus always tended to center on your flaws and failures. The positive events, the compliments, the little triumphs got lost.

Today you'll review your first six entries and summarize in this journal all that you've learned about your strengths. Cover the high points, the qualities that are most important to you. As best you can, describe them with certainty and conviction. Rather than write that you're "pretty good" with your kids, a better entry would affirm that you are "warm and supportive." Also, it helps to be specific. Instead of noting that you're "sometimes assertive," a more accurate entry would describe you as "assertive to make sure things are done correctly at work."

Go ahead now and summarize what you've learned to this point.

_____

_____

_____

_____

_____

_____

_____

_____

_____

_____

Your Psychological
Self-Portrait: The Weaknesses

L ast week you examined many of your positive qualities across six
domains of life. But your critical inner voice isn't going to let you
get away with just looking at the positives. That inner voice, ever con-
scious of your flaws, is saying, "But what about this? What about that?"
And it's reminding you of a steady stream of mistakes and failures from
the past.

That's how the inner critic works. As soon as we find something
positive about ourselves, it's compelled to say, "But wait," and gives us
chapter and verse of all the balancing negatives. It's as if our inner critic
can't stand to see us feel good.

Why is this? What makes the inner critic so determined to bring us
down? There's one simple and sad reason. We grow up with a familiar—if painful—picture of ourselves painted by trauma and hundreds of
messages about our identity. And we are scared of anything that threat-
ens to change that picture—however positive it may be—because then
we wouldn't know who we are. We'd have no way to make sense of the
world. It's incredibly frightening to find out reality is very different than
we thought. And we'll often try hard not to face that new reality.

That's why our inner critic works overtime to undermine each positive. This negative contribution lets us continue to know ourselves as we always have—as a person who is wrong, bad, or unworthy.

Now to work. It's time to use your journal to examine (and perhaps reinterpret) some of the negatives you've always believed about yourself. For the next six days, we'll return to the six domains of life you examined last week. This time we'll look at the traits and qualities you don't like about yourself in each domain. But we're going to do something more than list the negatives. We'll apply four specific principles to reframe and rewrite each trait you identify.

Physical Appearance

In your journal today we'd like you to list the parts of your physical self that you don't like. Remember, everyone has faults. There's no one on earth who doesn't have plenty of things they wish were different about themselves. But your self-esteem can actually be strengthened by honestly facing rather than running away from your flaws.

Once you've completed a list of physical qualities you wish were different, we want you to do four things:

1. *Rewrite the item using nonpejorative language.* In other words, "fat thighs" should be changed to something like "heavier than ideal thighs." "Ugly beak nose" could be rewritten as "large, rounded nose." This technique may seem simplistic or silly, but it isn't. One of your inner critic's biggest weapons is brutal, condemning language. And your first task must be to de-fang and soften that language so it does less harm.

2. *Rewrite the item using accurate language.* Instead of "fat thighs," the accurate statement would be "twenty-two-inch thighs." Instead of "weak, ugly chin," the accurate statement would be "receding chin, about a half inch too far back." Notice that accurate language uses exact measurements and clear descriptions, not global judgments.

3. *Rewrite the item acknowledging an exception.* An exception, in a case of undesirable physical traits, might be a compliment you once received regarding this part of your body. Or a culture, perhaps a time, where this trait might be viewed as attractive. Consider whether there is someone, generally viewed as attractive, who also has this trait (think Barbra Streisand or Jennifer Lopez).

You won't find exceptions for every physical trait you don't like. But with a little thought, you'll find a few. So put them down.

4. *Rewrite the item acknowledging a balancing strength.* Is there a part of your body—ideally near the problematic one—that you feel better about? Perhaps even like? Include that now in your description. For example: "I have broad, thirty-eight-inch hips, probably no bigger than J-Lo's (and she does okay), but I also have strong, athletic thighs."

Go ahead now and use these four techniques to develop a new description for each physical trait you're not fond of.

• • • • • • • DAY TWO • • • • • • •
Relating to Others

Today you should make a list in your journal of things you wish were different about how you deal with other people. Think about the ways you express your feelings or needs, how you deal with conflict, give support, and so on.

When you've completed the list, we'd like you to rewrite the items using the four principles outlined for Day One:

1. *Eliminate pejorative language.*

2. *Make it specific and accurate—not general.* For example, describe the specific situations where you get angry rather than indict yourself as "way too angry."

3. *Look for exceptions.* Here you should identify the people and situations where the negative trait doesn't hold true. "I get angry at my boss, sister, and mother, but almost never at my kids or my friends."

4. *Look for balancing strengths.* For every flaw in your interpersonal behavior, look for a corresponding strength. "I get angry, but I get over it quickly. And I'm very supportive to people I care about."

Using these four principles, "I'm wimpy and unassertive" would be rewritten, "I'm not as assertive as I'd like (leaving out pejorative "wimpy") with my boss and authority figures (specific and accurate), but I'm good at saying what I want with my husband and kids (exceptions). And I'm good at working out disagreements if somebody brings them up (balancing strength)."

• • • • • • DAY THREE • • • • • •
How Others See You

Today you can describe in your journal some of the criticisms you've gotten from others. Then apply the four techniques to rewrite each one.

1. *Eliminate pejorative language.*

2. *Make the criticism specific to a particular situation, rather than a generality.*

3. *Look for exceptions where the criticism doesn't hold true.*

4. *Look for balancing strengths.*

If your mother-in-law once described you to someone as selfish, let's see how this would be revised:

"I tend to be overly focused on myself (leave out pejorative 'selfish'), usually when I'm with very controlling older family members (specific and accurate). But I'm very aware of my kids', my friend Sam's, and my brother's needs (exceptions). And people tell me I'm generous and affectionate (balancing strength)."

_____

_____

_____

_____

_____

_____

_____

_____

_____

How You Do on the Job (or at School)

Today your journaling should focus on things you wish you did better at work (or school). Then apply the four principles to revise each item.

A weakness such as "screwing up paperwork" could be written as "inaccuracies on reports (eliminate pejorative 'screw up') amount to one or two transposed numbers per report (specific and accurate). On the other hand, I rarely make mistakes on actual sales figures (exceptions), and I'm told my reports are well written and graphically easy to use (balancing strengths)."

• • • • • • DAY FIVE • • • • • •
Your Performance of Daily Tasks

Your journaling for the day centers on weaknesses you may have in handling daily tasks of life —health maintenance, hygiene, maintaining a good living environment, money management, caring for kids, food preparation, etc. Once again, you should apply the four principles to rewrite each item.

An entry such as "lousy housekeeper" needs to be rewritten. It could change to something like, "difficulty keeping up with dishes, clutter, and some shopping (leave out "lousy"; specific and accurate), but I do a big cleanup and shop once a week (exception), and I'm very good at keeping a budget, monitoring kids' homework, and keeping kids' favorite foods in stock (balancing strengths)."

_____

_____

_____

_____

_____

_____

_____

_____

_____

_____

_____

_____

_____

_____

_____

• • • • • • DAY SIX • • • • • • •
Mental Functioning

Today you'll journal about some of the things you wish were different about how you use your mind. As usual, apply the four principles to rewrite each item.

An entry such as "uncreative" could be rewritten as "not interested in the arts or in making things (accurate and specific), but I'm great at decorating my home, and I'm into modern dance (exception). I also have a very good head for finance and problem solving (balancing strengths)."

_____

_____

_____

_____

_____

_____

_____

_____

_____

_____

_____

_____

_____

_____

_____

_____

_____

Putting It All Together

It's time now to weave together your strengths and weaknesses into a clear, healthy self-description. For each of the six domains, write a brief summary that includes the main strengths you identified last week combined with some of the weaknesses you rewrote during the last six days. Here's an example summary for "relating to others":

"I give a lot of time and energy to my family, and I'm very affectionate with my kids. I get disappointed sometimes about how the house runs, and I can withdraw or be irritable for an hour or two. On the other hand, I often pitch in and solve the problem myself or organize one of our famous 'housekeeping parties.' I'm very assertive when it comes to protecting the kids. But I can be passive sometimes about money and schedule problems. An exception to that is I always make sure the bills are paid, and I get the kids to where they need to go. I always try to help when someone needs me. And while I'm defensive about criticism of my parenting or work habits, I have a good sense of humor that often defuses conflict and cheers people up."

Go ahead now and write your summaries. This will take some effort, but the fair and balanced self-description you create can make you much less vulnerable to your inner critic.

_____

_____

_____

_____

_____

_____

_____

_____

_____

The History of Your
Self-Esteem

When you look back on your childhood, there are hundreds of emotionally charged images and memories. A few of them are *self-defining*, meaning that the memory is closely allied with your core identity. It tells you who you are and how you should feel about yourself.

The classic example of a self-defining memory was described by a thirty-five-year-old cinematographer, who, at age eight, was sent away to live with her grandmother. "The first thing Grandma said to me was that I'd been 'too much' for my mother, and my mother was never going to get her life working with me around. Grandma's house was cold, full of spooky, old furniture. I felt like I'd been banished there because I was bad." Now this memory comes up again and again, a touchstone for this woman's conviction that she "can't do anything right" and that sooner or later people will abandon her.

People with wounded self-esteem often have a collection of childhood memories that seem to confirm or even prove that they are bad or unworthy. And they can rarely recall balancing experiences where they felt successful or valued. What's worse, many of the negative memories get linked, so if one of them is triggered, a whole flood of old "I'm bad" memories can wash over you.

Changing how you relate to childhood memories is a key step to improved self-esteem. This week we're going to ask that you do some psychological mining, digging for memories and moments when you felt good about yourself—when you recall being loved, appreciated, or reaching some goal. Sometimes this isn't easy because your memory may be biased toward the negative. Or it may be hard to find good moments in a difficult childhood. We understand. But this week's journal work remains crucial because it will help you recapture important moments that will, taken together, begin to redefine your sense of self.

Each day this week you're going to review a specific era of your childhood, looking for memories that strengthen feelings of worth.

• • • • • • DAY ONE • • • • • •
Birth Through Three Years Old

Much of your review of this era may involve stories you've heard about yourself rather than direct memories. Your mother said you were a sweet baby and had a "light-up-the-room" smile. Your sister said you were smart and curious, spending a long time examining how every object worked. It's important to put some effort into this. Think of experiences at home, then away from home. Review stories related by your mother, father, siblings, and other family.

Try to recall when you were spoken to or touched in a way that told you that you were important and cared for. Recall a time—a birthday or special event—when you were given attention or praise. While working in your journal, be sure to underline any memories that are recurrent for you, things you think about at least once a year or more. Also underline memories that spark some emotion—longing, sadness, love, and so on.

• • • • • • DAY TWO • • • • • •
Four Through Six Years Old

Now we come to an era when you may have more specific memories. This is a period where you entered kindergarten and then the first grade. What positive memories do you have about your relationships in school? About things you did well or were praised for? What positive feedback do you remember from teachers? From your parents? What good memories do you have about neighborhood friends?

Again, it's important to work a little at this. Review all the significant events and changes during this era, and actively search for the smallest sliver of memory that conveys a sense of being valued.

Don't be surprised if negative memories keep pushing up and trying to replace the positive ones. It wouldn't be unusual if you had five spontaneous negative memories for every positive event you recall. This is normal; it's your old self-portrait trying to reassert itself. It doesn't want you to change. Just keep working, looking for memories that make you feel okay. As you did on Day One, underline memories that are recurring or carry an emotional charge.

_____

_____

_____

_____

_____

_____

_____

_____

_____

_____

_____

• • • • • • DAY THREE • • • • • • •
Seven Through Ten Years Old

Now we're going to explore mid-childhood, when you were in grades two to five. Again, review events with parents and siblings at home; with teachers and kids at school; and most particularly, with friendships where you felt valued or liked. Also recall successes—things you achieved or skills you were good at. Think about praise you received.

Don't be surprised if there's a part of you that discounts every positive, that assumes any praise was phony, obligatory, or just manipulation. You'll have to push through these doubts to keep journaling about your positive experiences. We know that sometimes this isn't easy but try anyway. Also remember to underline recurring memories or ones that touch you emotionally.

• • • • • • DAY FOUR • • • • • • •
Eleven Through Fifteen Years Old

This is a period of change and challenge. It's when you hit early to mid-adolescence, grades five to ten. It's the era when you may have begun to explore your sexuality and when kids often struggle with parents over issues of privacy and autonomy. During this time, you may have begun a relationship with your first girl- or boyfriend. As you have on previous days, journal about times when you felt valued, liked, or cared for by others. Remember moments of success; remember praise.

A lot of things were difficult during this era, and those memories will come up. But your task is to push through them to every moment and every relationship where you felt even a little good about yourself. Remember to underline memories that are either emotionally touching or recurring.

_____

_____

_____

_____

_____

_____

_____

_____

_____

_____

_____

_____

_____

_____

DAY FIVE
Sixteen Through Twenty Years Old

This is the era of late high school and early college. It may also cover the period when you first left home or had your first real job. Continue as you've been doing, journaling about positive experiences and positive relationships. Include goals you set, challenges you met, watershed events, and small moments where you were acknowledged or appreciated.

It's okay to include positive times and elements in an otherwise difficult situation. For example, your boyfriend may have valued your creative ability, even though you fought constantly and broke up because he plagiarized your papers. For most of us, adolescence is a bit of a nightmare, so don't be discouraged if many painful memories come up. We'll deal with them next week. For now, your task is to examine, carefully and thoroughly, these days of emerging independence to retrieve what was good in them. Remember to underline memories that are recurring or emotionally evocative.

• • • • • • DAY SIX • • • • • •
Surprises and Significant Memories

Review what you've written in your journal so far this week. What memories had the strongest emotional impact? Which recurring memories seem most connected to your identity? What do these key memories—the recurring and emotional ones—tell you about yourself? What can they teach you about your worth?

• • • • • • • DAY SEVEN • • • • • • •
Putting It All Together

Once again, read over this week's journal. But this time pretend you've discovered these lost pages on a park bench or in a subway car. Read them with curiosity—but without preconceptions. How do you feel about the stranger who wrote these words? What kind of person are they? Based only on the journal, what do you appreciate most about this person?

New Ways to See
Your Childhood

This week we're going to continue looking back at your childhood—but now the focus will be on memories that seem to support your old, negative self-portrait. You might wonder why we're encouraging you to remember these painful experiences. After all, if this journal is about building self-esteem, why would you return to early scenes of failure or rejection? The reason is because children make up things. Not the events themselves—they often recall those with pinpoint accuracy. But they frequently interpret memories through what we call the *I'm-bad filter*.

The I'm-bad filter distorts your history in three ways. First, it assumes that painful childhood events were your fault. You brought them on yourself by being willful or selfish or stupid. Second, it interprets cruelty and pain as punishments for your sins. All the mean things people have done to you are a payback for your flaws. Third, the filter suggests that happy, good times are undeserved, and your lot in life is to be forever slammed by rejection and failure.

When a child sees the world through the I'm-bad filter, even abusive behavior is considered reasonable. Even the most damaging attacks feel justified.

Your work this week is to learn to see the past without the filter. Painful childhood events are not payback, but rather evidence that growing up is inescapably difficult for most of us. Difficult things happened because kids are frequent victims of a world that clatters along indifferent to their feelings and needs. Bad things didn't happen because you are bad—they happened because the world is full of sharp edges that cut and bruise and wound children. That is the truth.

In your journal this week you'll learn to see your past in a new way—with awareness and empathy for how hard it is to grow up.

• • • • • • DAY ONE • • • • • •
Birth Through Three Years Old

Today in your journal we'd like you to again review your first three years, this time focusing on experiences that seem to confirm your negative self-image. Write down things you remember—or were told—that convey a sense that you were bad, wrong, or somehow displeasing to others. This period was a long time ago, and many of your memories will be hazy. Just do the best you can to recall anything that fits your old self-portrait.

But there's something else you need to do. For every negative memory you retrieve, you should ask yourself five questions:

1. *Was this normal behavior for my age?* In other words, is this what a lot of kids do when they're very little? For example, having a tantrum or throwing food is developmentally normal for a two-year-old. No matter how annoying it might be for parents or caretakers, it's still normal.

2. *Was my behavior determined by the circumstances?* Did the situation require or in some way push you to respond as you did? Keep in mind that you were a child, and what happened in your world was very much controlled by the big people around you. Honestly evaluate whether you had much choice about your behavior.

3. *Was my behavior a way to cope?* Did it help you deal with a frightening or difficult situation? For example, a three-year-old who's obstinate and always saying no to things may be living in a world where no one listens to the child's needs or feelings.

4. *Is there a different explanation for what happened—other than being bad?* How would you explain what happened if it were someone else? Are there alternative ways to interpret your behavior?

5. *Was there something positive in my behavior?* Is there anything about this memory that highlights your strengths—for example, your ability to survive? Was there something good that came out of your response in this situation?

Go ahead right now and apply these five questions to each specific memory. Then use your journal to explore your answers.

• • • • • • DAY TWO • • • • • •
Four Through Six Years Old

Today you will be recalling events during the period when you first started school. These are things you did or were done to you that gave you a feeling of being bad or wrong. These memories may be more glaring and easier to find than the positive experiences you explored last week. That's normal—particularly when a person struggles with low self-esteem.

Finding a negative memory is only the first step. Now evaluate each memory using the five questions you tried out yesterday. Then write in your journal how that memory might look or feel different in light of those questions.

Not all questions will apply to a particular memory, but at least a few of them will. Try to honestly explore how your *interpretation* of the memory might change as you think about what was normal, what was a survival or coping strategy, what was determined by circumstances, etc.

_____

_____

_____

_____

_____

_____

_____

_____

_____

_____

_____

_____

_____

_____

_____

_____

• • • • • • DAY THREE • • • • • • •
Seven Through Ten Years Old

Now you're about to explore memories when you were in grades two to five. Review experiences at home and school, with family and friends. While these memories will feel initially negative, you should carefully evaluate each one using the five questions. Then use your journal to write about what you learn.

• • • • • • DAY FOUR • • • • • • •
Eleven Through Fifteen Years Old

Today the focus is on mid-adolescence: grades five through ten. A lot of people remember both peer and dating relationships during the high school years as painful. This is a tough period for almost everybody, and you're likely to find a fair number of negative memories in this era.

Be sure to apply the five questions to each memory and record in your journal what you learn. While the memories themselves won't change, in many cases your interpretation of the memory will.

• • • • • • DAY FIVE • • • • • • •
Sixteen Through Twenty Years Old

Today you'll focus on memories from the late high school through early college period. This is the era when you probably left home for the first time and when you had your first significant jobs. As you've done throughout the week, use the five questions to reevaluate each memory. Write down what you discover.

• • • • • • DAY SIX • • • • • • •
The I'm-Bad Filter

Which of the five questions was most helpful for reinterpreting your past? Which gave you the best perspective from which to see your childhood differently? Use your journal to explore some of the ways your viewpoint has shifted. In particular, how has the I'm-bad filter changed for the memories you explored this week?

• • • • • • DAY SEVEN • • • • • •
Surprises

Review what you've written in your journal so far this week. What memories surprised you most as you explored them with the five questions? How did your old, negative assumptions change as you examined those memories? In what way (large or small) has your thinking about the past shifted during this week?

_____

_____

_____

_____

_____

_____

_____

_____

_____

_____

_____

_____

_____

_____

_____

_____

_____

_____

_____

Ending the Tyranny
of Shoulds

There are messages that you inherit from parents, peers, religion, or community that fuel "should" statements in your mind. These "shoulds" become a barometer against which you compare yourself. When you fail to live up to your shoulds, you chastise yourself, and think things like "I should have done better," "I should always be happy, never sad or depressed," "I should be more productive," or "I should be a perfect friend/relative/lover." This week you'll figure out what shoulds you hold yourself accountable to.

You may mistake these should sentiments for motivation. You may believe these shoulds are helping you to strive to become a better person. But shoulds are actually destructively rigid, establishing impossible guideposts to live by. Shoulds cause you to feel inadequate, ashamed, hopeless, or frustrated. This isn't a productive process—it's simply beating yourself up.

One way to stop shoulds from controlling your life is to separate shoulds from authentic values. Values can provide meaning and purpose—they help you reach inside yourself and encourage you to do what is right and important to you. Here's how you can tell the difference between a should and a healthy value. Healthy values are:

1. *Flexible, allowing for exceptions depending on the circum-stances.* Unhealthy shoulds are unbending and universally applied.

2. *Owned rather than obligatory.* Owning a value means you've critically examined this rule and have consciously chosen it. An obligatory should—often inherited from parents or family—can cause you to do something because you feel you ought to, and not because it fits with your personal needs, goals, and experience of life.

3. *Realistic, based on an assessment of positive versus negative consequences.* Realistic values usually lead to a positive outcome. The purpose of this value is to lead to something that feels good. An unrealistic should would tell you to pursue something "because it's right," regardless of the costs or negative outcomes. For example, it would be unrealistic to stay in a bad marriage just because one "shouldn't" divorce. The emotional consequences, stretched over many years, would be catastrophic—all to comply with some rule that doesn't make sense.

4. *Life-enhancing rather than life-restricting.* Your values should allow you to pursue your emotional, intellectual, and physical needs. They shouldn't force you to sacrifice things that are crucial to your well-being.

There are plenty of opportunities in life to push yourself and to strive to be better. You can find healthy ways to motivate yourself based on your core values.

Shoulds attack your self-esteem in two ways. First, the passed-down rules may not fit you. They drive you to compare yourself to some ideal of perfection. When you fail this impossible test, your self-esteem becomes the victim and is damaged by this harsh inner critic.

For example, suppose your family's work ethic meant that as a man, your role was providing for your family, regardless of the cost to your personal fulfillment. This meant absolute self-sacrifice. But you choose work that feeds your artistic nature, even though this work earns less. Your should goes after your self-esteem, chastising you for not bringing in all the money you could. You beat yourself up with thoughts like, "I shouldn't care so much about my own needs. I should be thinking about my wife and kids first and foremost. I'm selfish and childish for pursuing something only because it 'matters' to me."

You have a right to be both personally satisfied *and* responsible. The should is holding you to an ideal that doesn't fit who you are. This should is life restricting and obligatory rather than life enhancing and chosen.

The second way shoulds attack self-esteem is to go after you on moral grounds. That is, your shoulds may have a built-in implication of right and wrong in situations that are completely unrelated to moral values. For example, if your parents insisted that your personal tastes—clothing, music, friends—were "wrong," you may end up with shoulds that turn matters of taste and preference into a moral issue.

This week you'll learn to recognize which shoulds have become critical rules that end up making you feel badly about yourself. You'll begin by listing all of the shoulds that come to mind. You'll go on to challenge damaging, unhealthy shoulds so that they become more flexible and realistic. You'll also identify values that are healthy guidelines that you want and choose to live by.

Discovering Your Shoulds

Today you'll write down a list of your personal shoulds. Write them as they come into your mind, don't censor or second-guess yourself. Today is just about writing whatever comes up for you when you ask yourself, "What are my rules for living?"

Shoulds often govern how you act in relationships ("I should always be a patient, giving lover"), set standards for success and achievement ("I should have gotten an MBA" or "I should take more initiative at work"), and tell you how to parent ("My children should always be happy; I should give them all of my time"). Some other typical shoulds that you might have inherited can be centered on values such as commitment, honesty, generosity, dignity, intelligence, or strength. You might have a voice in you head (often called an *automatic thought*) that assigns negative labels such as selfish, weak, lazy, or stupid.

Make a list of should statements that have become the rules in life you feel you ought to live by.

_____

_____

_____

_____

_____

_____

_____

_____

_____

_____

_____

Why Are They Unhealthy?

Today is a step toward having healthier values, ones that are not so hurtful and damaging to your self-esteem. Look back at your list from yesterday and choose three should statements that you believe undermine your self-esteem. For example, select those that cause you undue guilt or shame, inner conflict (you can tell you don't agree with the should), or are driven by intense obligation (not choice).

Write down each of these three should statements. Below each, explore how it does or doesn't meet each of the four criteria listed at the beginning of this chapter.

1. *Inflexible and rigid.* Does the should permit no reasonable exceptions? Does the language of your should include absolutes such as "always" and "never"?

2. *Life restricting rather than life enhancing.* Has the should restricted your choices? Did you have to let go of things you really wanted to comply with it? Give examples.

3. *Obligatory rather than owned.* Does the should feel like something required of you by others, a rule you've inherited from parents or mentors? Have you ever examined it and claimed it as your own? Describe where the should comes from and how it does or doesn't fit your deepest personal values.

4. *Unrealistic.* Explore what happens when you apply the should to a specific situation or choice. List the positive and negative outcomes of making a decision based on a should.

_____

_____

_____

• • • • • • DAY THREE • • • • • •
Where Would You Be
Without Those Shoulds?

If the should doesn't fit you, you have to be rid of it. You have to stop punishing yourself and feeling guilty. What would your life be like if you changed or let go of the shoulds you explored yesterday? Think back to some of the significant points of decision in your life. What might you have done differently? How might you have felt differently? What about right now? Are there things you're doing or not doing that are influenced by these shoulds? What choices might you make differently if your shoulds became more flexible and life-affirming?

• • • • • • DAY FOUR • • • • • • •
Identifying Your Healthy Values

Now that you've rewritten these important shoulds, let's begin to clarify how you really do want to live your life. What's important to you? What are your authentic values? Healthy values are yours—they fit how you see the world, they support the things that are most important to you, they take care of the ones you love.

Today, think of someone who you deeply admire. Maybe this person is someone you think of when you feel indecisive, perhaps imagining what they would do in your situation. In certain ways, this person may personify your core values. What you respect in them points to what you deem to be most important.

Write about this person. When you think of them, what qualities stand out? Try to list these qualities. Why do you admire them? Last and most important, which of them do you share?

• • • • • • DAY FIVE • • • • • • •
Your Healthy Values

Pursuing healthy values can boost your sense of purpose and meaning in life. And making choices based on healthy values can boost your self-esteem. Identify one of your core values to pay attention to today. What are the positive ways you express this healthy value with your family or partner? At work or school? Why is this value important to you?

For example, if you value reliability, you'd write down specific ways in which you have lived up to this value over the years.

Also note how the value is healthy: is it flexible, realistic, life-enhancing, and claimed by you? At the end of the exercise, go back to Day One of this week and underline your key healthy values.

_____

_____

_____

_____

_____

_____

_____

_____

_____

_____

_____

_____

_____

_____

_____

• • • • • • • DAY SIX • • • • • • •
Personal Passions

What inspires your passions? Do you have any talents you cherish, that make you feel excited or proud? Is it important that you spend time nurturing this talent, skill, or form of enjoyment? Do you enjoy painting, gardening, reading poetry, or writing short fiction? Or perhaps you find being in nature restorative and important in life. Write about the love you have for the activity. What are your favorite aspects of the activity, and how does it make you feel? Do you make time in your day/week/month to pursue what matters to you personally? How can you insure this time for yourself?

Values and Self-Esteem

Some values are harder to sustain than others. At times, following your values might upset other people— they may not like what you're standing for. Commitment to values comes at a cost sometimes. Living by healthy values can be hard work. But when you manage it, you gain a sense of rightness, that you've done something difficult and important. Today you'll describe some instances when you've followed healthy values.

Think of times that your values have motivated you to keep up with the hard work of life: self-improvement, pursuing more education, raising a family, going for a promotion, and so on. Recall times you've been willing to persevere because your values stand for something greater than just the hard work. Describe a situation in which you suffered through something because you believed it was worth it—you stuck with it because of something you value.

Perhaps you value ideals such as being personally aware; understanding the world; having a loving, functioning family; or working hard to achieve your potential. Living a value-driven life can sustain and improve your self-esteem because you're doing things that matter to you, that you believe in. Today think of one core value that helps you feel better about yourself.

For example: "I value a healthy relationship in which we express love and support for each other. Sometimes this means sticking with it when we have a disagreement. We had a fight last night about our differing political opinions, and I was frustrated. I wanted to storm out of the room, telling him to cram his lame brain ideas where the sun don't shine. But I value our love and our communication, so I took a deep breath and listened. I tried to respect his opinion, even if I didn't agree. By the end of the night, we'd resolved our fight. I came out of it knowing it was worth being patient and really listening, because I value this relationship. Being a part of the resolution made me feel good about myself—I could actually feel my self-esteem improve."

Think of stories you hear about the early labor movement, when workers had to unite and fight for what they valued—fair wages, healthier conditions, etc. Those people risked everything in order to defend their values.

Think of a time when you had to speak up in a group and were the lone voice defending an idea most opposed. It could have been at work or school, in a religious setting, or with family. Describe the effort you made because you believed in something more important that made the difficulty worthwhile. Write about how it felt to stand up for something meaningful to you.

The Power of
Thoughts

Inside each one of us is a constant monologue of thoughts. This is normal. It's what we do to explain and interpret the world around us. Sometimes the monologue is nothing more than labeling experiences: "big car . . . cold . . . yard needs water . . . flaming sunset." Sometimes the monologue maliciously attacks us, turning each event of our lives into an indictment of our worth.

The trouble with the inner monologue, and the reason it can exert such a powerful influence, is that we usually don't notice it. Not consciously. It drifts, like a misty waterfall, down the back of our mind. Though we seldom recognize it, the monologue gives us a steady flow of negative messages about who we are and what we do. And, over months and years of listening, we believe it.

Whatever the monologue says always seems true. No matter how absurd or exaggerated. That's because we mistake it for authentic sensory experience. When we think to ourselves, "I'm stupid," it seems just as real as thinking, "It's hot." But the two thoughts aren't the same. One is a label for what your senses tell you; one is an overgeneralized conclusion that distorts reality.

So the monologue often lies, especially if you already have injured self-esteem. And it employs some very clever strategies. It will compare you to people who have skills or accomplishments you lack. It will make you filter reality so you see only the negative. The monologue will fill you with regret for past failures, or exaggerate your current ones. It will mind-read that others are judging you and blame you for anything that goes wrong.

Your monologue is steady and insidious. Every day it's working at tearing you down. It uses the words and labels your parents often used. Or a lover who left you. Or your third grade teacher who hated you from day one. The words seem certain and clear—like they were written on the tablets at Sinai. But, in reality, they are lies, repeated like some Joseph Goebels propaganda, until they seem as true as gray clouds or blue sky.

It doesn't have to be this way. Remember, the power of the monologue is that it's psychologically invisible. When you start to notice what it says and how it works, it loses much of its ability to inflict harm. So the first thing you'll do this week is pay attention. Really listen to that inner voice. Then you'll question it, examining the truth of what it says. Finally, you'll learn to distance from it. You'll listen as if the monologue was someone else's voice, something you notice but no longer believe.

• • • • • • DAY ONE • • • • • •
Comparing

Today the focus is on one of the most vicious ways your inner monologue can attack—by comparing you to others. You find someone who is more competent or more accomplished in a specific area and crucify yourself with the comparison. In effect, you're picking a fight that you're trying to lose. But here's the thinking error that underlies this self-attack: *selective attention*. You're choosing to compare only the qualities where you come up short. There are skills and abilities where you would be superior—or at least as good. And there are plenty of other people you'd compare well to.

Write about a recent experience where you were caught up in comparing. Describe the situation, what you thought and felt. Now look at the other side. How might you stack up well with this person? What are you proud of in yourself that remains true regardless of the ways others might shine?

Now give yourself some distance from the painful comparison. It's just a thought, nothing more. It's not important; it doesn't change anything. See the thought getting smaller. Put the thought on a leaf and let it drift away downstream. Further, further, out of sight. Write in your journal about how it feels to think it now.

• • • • • • • DAY TWO • • • • • • •
Filtering

Today we want you to pay attention to a process called filtering. When you filter, your inner monologue only talks about the negative—about your flaws and failures. Meanwhile, your strengths are ignored. Your accomplishments remain invisible. As with comparing, the thinking error that underlies filtering is selective attention. You are ignoring a huge part of reality—your positive experience.

Write about a recent experience where you got trashed by your inner monologue. Describe the situation, what you thought or felt. Now look at some of the balancing realities. What strengths offset the weakness you focused on? In what similar situations have you succeeded? Is there anything about the problem situation that you handled well? What are you proud of in yourself that remains true, regardless of this problem situation?

Now build emotional distance from your negative thoughts. These are nothing more than transitory ideas—they are not important. They are lies because they leave out big parts of who you are. See the thoughts getting smaller. Put the thoughts on a leaf and let them float away downstream. Further, further, out of sight. Write in your journal about any changes you've noticed in these thoughts.

Regrets

Pathological regret is a key strategy for your negative inner voice. You find yourself caught in sadness and self-attack over a choice you made in the past. "That was stupid . . . that was wrong . . . you really screwed that up," says the voice. "Look at the pain you caused . . . look at what you lost," it nags.

The thinking error underlying pathological regret is twenty-twenty *hindsight*. The mistake can only be recognized as such with the perfect awareness that comes from looking back. At the time of the choice, if you are completely honest about your hopes, fears, and how you saw things, you probably did the best you could. You chose what seemed reasonable at the time. Only in retrospect does the choice become wrong.

Today, in your journal, we'd like you to explore a situation you regret. But this time really look at it as you did at the time—what you feared, what you expected, what you knew and didn't know, what you hoped for. Climb into your head as you made the decision; be the person you were then. Now explore this question: did you do the best you could with what you knew and understood at the time?

Try to open some emotional distance from this regret. This was a sad moment in your life, but it is in the past. Accept that you did the best you knew how to do, and accept the pain of what was lost. Take a breath and pull away, letting the moment take its place among all the events of your life—one of many. Write in your journal any changes you experience in how you feel about this regret.

_____

_____

_____

_____

_____

• • • • • • • DAY FOUR • • • • • • •
Exaggerating

Today you'll explore a process that's familiar to all of us, but one that can savage self-esteem: exaggeration. Your negative inner voice uses exaggeration in two ways. First, it overgeneralizes. Your monologue will say things like: "You *always* make mistakes . . . you *never* do anything to help your mother . . . *everyone* thinks you're selfish . . . *no one* enjoys being with you."

Notice how the words "always," "never," "everyone," and "no one" tend to exaggerate a problem, and, through selective attention, ignore all the times when you've done well.

The second form of exaggeration is magnifying. You describe things to yourself as "horrible," "awful," "disgusting," etc. The hyperbole is rarely true because it ignores parts of the experience that aren't awful or horrible.

Write about a recent event that your inner monologue exaggerated. Describe what happened and what you thought and felt without overgeneralizing or magnifying. Try to be accurate and objective, as if you were writing a newspaper report.

Now put the event in perspective. You've been through many hard moments in your life. This was one of them. But you've also had moments of success and accomplishment—moments to be proud of. Write about how this event looks in the context of your life as a whole.

• • • • • • • DAY FIVE • • • • • • •
Mind Reading

Your critical inner voice has another potent weapon—mind reading. Here you assume knowledge of how other people see and judge you. All your vicious self-criticism is projected; you imagine that folks feel and react the same way you do. "He thinks I made a fool of myself . . . she's bored with my conversation . . . he thinks I'm ugly . . . she's horrified by things in my past." The thinking error built into mind reading is called *arbitrary inference*—forming beliefs about others without evidence.

Write about a recent experience where you made an assumption about how others were judging you. Describe the events, as well as what you thought and felt. Explore what actual evidence you had for what you assumed. Can you imagine alternative things—either positive or neutral—the other person might reasonably have thought? Looking back, does your mind reading feel accurate, or does it feel more like a projection of your negative voice?

Now give yourself a little distance from this painful experience. The assumptions you made may or may not be true. Let it be in doubt; let it be uncertain. You have no way of knowing for sure what someone thinks unless you ask them. Drift further from the pain; let it take its place in the past. Let it shrink in size and importance. Write in your journal about how this experience feels now.

• • • • • • DAY SIX • • • • • •
Self-Blame

Have you noticed how your negative inner voice likes to blame you for everything, whether you're at fault or not? When something goes wrong, it's usually traced back to some error on your part. The habit of self-blame is built on a thinking error called the *fallacy of control*. It's the idea that you're omnipotent; that you have 100 percent power over everything that happens. This is pretty silly when you look at it. Every event stands at the end of long chains of cause and effect. You may contribute to the outcome but are rarely totally responsible. And sometimes you aren't responsible at all.

Write about a recent experience where you blame yourself for something. Describe what occurred, what you thought and felt. Now describe all that contributed to the event—the behavior and choices of everyone who was part of it. Don't forget to look at environmental or circumstance factors—how did these affect the outcome? Also explore your moment of choice—what did you know, fear, or hope for as you made the decision you now regret?

How responsible do you feel now? Have you blamed yourself for others' behavior? When you try to be objective, how much of the outcome really belongs to you? Now pull back from this experience. It's a sad event that probably has multiple causes. See it as one of many, many moments in your life. Accept how disappointing it is, how much you wish things were different. Let it recede further and further. Let it take its place among your regrets and successes. Write about how this experience feels right now.

_____

_____

_____

_____

_____

_____

• • • • • • DAY SEVEN • • • • • • •
Integration

In your journal, write what you've learned about your inner monologue and how it affects you. Which of the six strategies we've explored so far seems most relevant to you? Which of the many countermeasures you explored this week seems most useful? Do you feel ready to start talking back to your inner monologue? What do you plan to say when it attacks?

Living by Your
Own Truth

Y ou have a truth that lives inside of you. Your truth is your "gut reaction." It's your silent sense of things, or the loud, screaming voice inside of you dying to express itself. The more you give words to your inner voice and live by your own truth, the more control you'll have to make your own decisions and follow your own path.

Communicating your truth is a major first step. Being assertive allows you to stand up for your worth by stating your opinions, asking for what you need, and telling people what you think and feel. Being assertive means you act as if you deserve to be heard, as if the worth you sometimes doubt in yourself is absolute and obvious. If your destination is self-esteem, assertiveness is a highway that will get you there.

Assertiveness is the balance point between submissiveness, where you're afraid to communicate anything at all, and aggressiveness, which is more about attacking and demanding than asking for what you want. In between these two is a place where you speak your mind with clear and respectful messages.

There are probably moments when you feel your truth, but something prohibits its expression. Some typical barriers to assertiveness include feeling:

- Nervous about imposing on others;

- Uncomfortable bringing attention to yourself and your needs;

- Worried that others won't like or approve of what you have to say;

- You must be wrong or will sound stupid (self-doubt);

- You will alienate people who like you because you are typically "nice."

These barriers grow from what others need, not what you need. This week, you'll learn skills to help you move past these barriers successfully. You'll develop tools to help you live by your own truth.

Living by your own truth provides an enormous boost to your self-esteem because it tells the world that you believe in yourself. This week you'll focus on the following six vital areas: telling others what you believe, communicating how you feel, revealing what harms you, telling what you want, saying no, and sharing with others goals you're setting for your life.

At first, telling, asking, and receiving may feel like a luxury that you don't deserve. It's probably almost instinctual at this point to defer to others' needs and opinions and to overlook your own. You may immediately assume that someone else is right before you've even voiced your perspective. You may not be used to asking for things such as understanding, respect, or empathy. But you can learn to live with this discomfort as you begin to be heard and have your needs met.

At first the trick is just to *act* as if you deserve these things. But over time, by changing your behaviors, you can begin to build your self-esteem from the outside in. It's okay if standing up for yourself doesn't feel natural at first. Just ease into it. With the writing exercises, you can take baby steps. You will be able to recall times when expressing yourself worked and imagine how it could work in the future.

Telling What You Believe

When you tell people what you believe, you're sharing your unique perspective. No one else sees things the way you do. Your interpretation of reality is made up of your understanding of a situation, your past experiences, and your unique sensitivities. Today you'll write about a belief you want to communicate but feel apprehensive about sharing. You're going to write out an imaginary scenario in which you tell someone exactly what you believe, using these key skills:

- Describe one or two events or facts that support your belief.

- Describe your belief in simple, direct language.

- Avoid sarcasm or any expression of contempt or judgment regarding contrary beliefs.

- Invite feedback and alternative opinions.

- Respectfully acknowledge opinions and beliefs of others.

If someone in this scenario disagrees with your assertion, try to show flexibility: "Interesting point. That's something worth thinking about."

Now write about the situation in which you wish you could use these skills. The writing you do today can function as a kind of script. As you think through the scenario, you'll be preparing yourself to express your belief in real life. In fact, once you have the script, practice using it front of a mirror. Try to imagine that you're addressing the person you've written about in your script.

_____

_____

_____

_____

● ● ● ● ● ● ● DAY TWO ● ● ● ● ● ● ●
Communicating How You Feel

Today is about telling other people how you feel. It can seem much easier to discount your own feelings rather than risk being rejected or misunderstood. But inhibiting your emotional expression can lead to bottled-up resentments, a lack of joy, and even a disconnection from yourself. Telling people how you feel opens a door that allows you to build intimacy, connection, and understanding. Remember, your feelings are not judgments or accusations—they're just your feelings. "I feel excited about this change," or "I feel lonely when you're on business trips."

One of the most useful skills in telling people how you feel is to distinguish between facts and feelings. First describe the facts, following them with a statement about how you feel about those facts. When creating this "facts-plus-feelings" statement make sure to:

- Describe the actual triggering event;

- Use nonpejorative language;

- Omit opinions or judgments.

Then, when describing how you feel about those facts:

- Use simple "I" statements (avoid saying "Anyone would be upset by that"; rather, "I felt upset by that");

- Avoid disguised opinions. For example, instead of "I feel that you're a rude person" say "I felt offended by that comment."

Today write about the feeling you want to tell someone about. Create your script using the facts-plus-feelings format. Practice in front of a mirror or with someone you feel safe with.

_____

_____

• • • • • • DAY THREE • • • • • •
Revealing What Harms You

Telling someone when something harms you is part of building a sense of wholeness and self-esteem. Your pain is an integral part of who you are, and telling others about it is an important part of really living by your truth.

Harm includes something that damages your health or sense of worth, something that stresses or exhausts you, or something that prevents your needs from being met. Harm can also come from someone who's angry and attacking or someone who violates your boundaries (for instance, betrays your confidence or saps your time and energy). Harm can result when someone expects things of you that prevent you from meeting important needs, like a boss who expects you to work so much overtime that you miss out on most social or family time. A partner who unreasonably limits you and restricts your freedom is causing you harm.

Today, write about someone who causes you harm. Describe the situation in your journal and write out a scenario in which you tell this person exactly how you're being harmed. Your key skills for communicating this are to:

- Describe the problem in nonpejorative language.

- Keep your tone of voice steady and flat.

- Describe the specific ways the problem affects you.

• • • • • • DAY FOUR • • • • • • •
Telling Others What You Need

What you need usually stems from your deeper physical, emotional, intellectual, and spiritual needs. When something is important to you, you have every right to ask for it. It doesn't matter what others think—what matters is knowing that your needs are worthy of speaking aloud.

Be specific about what you need (help, time, affection,) and how you'd like this need fulfilled (help after work, time alone next Saturday). "I really need your help weeding the front yard this weekend," or "I'd like you to pay more attention to me after work," or "I want to spend time alone this evening." Assume that your needs are legitimate and that you have every right to have this need. Don't apologize for what you want, just make the request with clarity.

Today write about something you want. Who do you need to communicate this to? Here are your skills for telling someone what you want:

- Don't apologize.

- Be specific.

- Ask for behavioral rather than attitudinal change ("I'd like you to visit Mom with me this weekend" rather than "I need you to like my mother more").

- Ask for one thing at a time.

_____

_____

_____

_____

_____

_____

_____

• • • • • • DAY FIVE • • • • • •
Saying No

When you're able, you can give. But when you've reached maximum capacity, you can say no. It's this simple. Your personal limits are invisible to others, known only by you. They include how much you can give and when, to whom, in what capacity, and how often. Giving beyond your means will often leave you feeling exploited, hurting your self-esteem.

The truth is, many people in your life may not be used to you making your limits clear, and they may not necessarily like it. After all, they're probably accustomed to you giving freely whenever they need it. But when you are maxed out, it's your responsibility to yourself to say no. Drawing this line can seem scary at first, but there are good ways to say no in any situation. Don't defend yourself or make excuses when it isn't necessary. And it helps to make direct eye contact and keep your voice calm and steady.

Today write about the person you want to say no to, but haven't. Write down what you want to say, and how. Right now you're just practicing for the moment when your opportunity to say no arises. Practice makes perfect, and by working on it now, you'll be ready when the instance comes up. These are your skills for saying no:

- Be clear in your mind about your right to protect and take care of yourself.

- Describe your limits.

- Say no firmly, in a strong voice.

- Offer no justifications or apologies.

- Describe in your journal how you'll take care of yourself if your limit is not respected. These are the consequences of someone not listening to your clear statement.

If you need to, practice saying no in the mirror. Watch your facial expressions and remember how important body language, eye contact, and tone are when you're telling someone no.

• • • • • • DAY SIX • • • • • • •
Setting Your Life Course

Setting and achieving goals in life is an important part of living by your truth because you are choosing to pursue what you need in your life. Accomplishing these goals helps you to feel good about your ability to get things done that are important to you.

To help define your goals, think about areas of life that you feel passionately about. These may include family, career, your love life, or your creative endeavors. For our purposes, your goals may be big and life changing or simply fun. There are no right or wrong answers. Maybe you've always wanted to learn to sew, to knit, or to join a book group. Perhaps you have wanted to move up to a position of leadership in your career. How could you take the steps necessary to reach these goals?

Today write about your direction in life. Identify where you'd like to be headed:

- Get clear about what matters to you.

- Describe each goal and the initial steps you need to take.

- Share your goal with everyone it will affect.

• • • • • • DAY SEVEN • • • • • •
Living Your Truth

This week you paid attention to six very important areas of your self-esteem. You wrote about ways you're going to stand up for your feelings, assert your needs, and meet your goals in successful ways. You know these things are possible and are the right thing to do. After all, you know that speaking up for yourself means you're paying attention to what is true for you. It's a way to value yourself—and that's what self-esteem is about.

Today, write about how your life could be different if you behaved assertively with other people. Can you see how saying what you think and feel means living your own truth? For example, does saying no assert clear boundaries? Would this ease tension you feel when others need something from you because you know you can say no? How will voicing your inner truth help you build a healthy sense of self-esteem? Does it give you more personal power and control over your life? Do you like this picture of yourself? Is this an ideal you'd like to pursue?

_____

_____

_____

_____

_____

_____

_____

_____

_____

_____

_____

The Achilles Heel

The Achilles heel is the most vulnerable area of your self-worth. It's your weakness. It could be in relationships, with authority, family, or whatever. When you're there, you know it. You feel like you're sinking. Suddenly you get flooded by a feeling of shame, or self-dislike, and all of the lessons you've learned about holding onto a positive self-image seem to disappear or dissolve.

You're not alone—even the most competent, self-assured person has an Achilles heel. This chapter is going to teach you how to recognize what triggers your Achilles heel and how to find your core power in those moments.

The Achilles-heel experience usually feels like it comes out of the blue. It's as if you're walking along feeling fairly confident, aware of your strengths, and then suddenly you step into a rabbit hole and plummet into a pit of confusion. The triggering event may have been a criticism or rejection of some kind. All you know is that you're drowning, and all you feel is self-doubt. All memories of your worth, skill, and achievement vanish.

When you feel this way, there's a two-part process occurring. First, there is an event, such as criticism or a mistake you made. Second, the event taps into a negative core belief, a deep-seated conviction that you're unworthy in some way. Prime examples include the belief that you're incompetent, or that people won't really love you. You come to a conclusion, based on the event coupled with the negative core belief, such as "I always screw up!" or "I've failed as a parent!" It's when these three are combined that you can feel devastated. A triggering event that doesn't tap into a negative core belief won't lead you to that awful conclusion. Neither will the negative core belief without a triggering event. When all three gang up on you, strategies for noticing what is good about yourself become elusive and distant.

Some classic core beliefs are:

- I'm unlovable.

- I'll never have the support or nourishment I need.

- I'll never succeed.

- I'm not smart or capable.

- I'm flawed and selfish.

- I'll be abandoned.

- I may look good on the outside, but inside I'm really worthless.

- I'm undeserving.

- I always end up hurting other people.

- I don't belong anywhere or really fit with anyone.

Negative core beliefs are kind of like your ticking time bomb. They sit there waiting for just the right event to set them off. For instance, suppose you have a core belief that you're basically not smart or capable. Ordinarily, you might be able to balance this belief with events in your life that prove you can accomplish tasks, projects, or schoolwork well. However, if you screw up somehow—a botched project at work, a bad grade, etc.—you'll leap to an extreme conclusion, "I'll never succeed! I'm such an idiot!" And then *pow*—the time bomb explodes. This is your

Achilles heel moment. You lose sight of a balanced picture of reality and plummet into the darkness of the rabbit hole.

You'll begin by writing about your five most insidious triggering events. On each of the following days, you'll figure out which core belief this event stimulates and develop tools for climbing out of the pit. There will be two parts to this process: First you'll collect evidence, memories, and experiences that will refute the conclusion you've drawn, and second, you'll distill this evidence into a positive statement that can immediately counterbalance that negative core belief. This statement will become what's known as an *affirmation*. It'll be like a cue card that you can pull out in any situation to help you find your balance again. No longer will you feel powerless when events bring on an Achilles heel moment. You'll understand what's happening to you, why, and how to take charge of the situation.

• • • • • • • DAY ONE • • • • • • •
Five Triggering Events

In your journal today we'd like you to write about five kinds of events that generally provoke the Achilles-heel experience. We're not talking about specific events here—you'll be exploring those later in the week. Today you simply list the sorts of things that usually bring out your Achilles heel. Below is a list of some types of events that tend to trigger most people. Choose five from the list and add any that apply to you but aren't on the list already.

- *Mistakes.* Times you missed a deadline or failed a test.

- *Criticism.* Someone tells you that you're doing something wrong.

- *Being exposed.* Someone has suddenly seen your hidden qualities.

- *Disappointment.* You miss out on something you've always wanted

- *Memories.* Significant memories of being hurt or hurting someone else.

- *Taking a risk.* Being promoted, taking on new responsibility and challenges.

- *Challenging authority.* Standing up for yourself with a supervisor, parent, or someone whose opinion matters to you.

Write down five intimidating events that seem to trip your Achilles heel. You'll learn how to handle each of these throughout the rest of this week.

_____

_____

_____

Challenging the First Event

Today choose the first one of your triggering events to work with. Remember a time when this experience made you feel like you just got laid out flat. Describe the event. What happened? How did it make you feel? For instance, did the event make you feel immense shame, as if you were nothing more than the mistake or criticism?

Now go back to the list of core beliefs and see if you can identify the core belief that this event triggered. Think about your core belief. What did the Achilles-heel experience lead you to think about yourself? The core belief causes painful thoughts, which is understandable, because this core belief is turning what should be a fairly neutral event into an Achilles heel nightmare.

But here's an important question: Is your core belief entirely true? Let's explore this. Let's see if there's any evidence from your past that contradicts the devastating Achilles-heel belief. For example, if your core belief is that you're not smart, look for specific memories that clearly mark your intelligence and capability. Recall as many exceptions to the core belief as you can think of. Now we'd like you to write a one-sentence summary of these exceptions. Phrase the sentence in a positive way so it becomes something of an affirmation. For example, "I know that I'm intelligent: I achieve mini-accomplishments every day that provide evidence of my intelligence. I balance our household budget, and I manage an efficient staff at work—and these are just two examples."

• • • • • • DAY THREE • • • • • • •

Challenging the Second Event

Today, you'll be working with the second Achilles-heel event, whether it's making mistakes, taking risks, or another you've identified. Recall a time that this Achilles heel came up. Remember what it felt like to be in the situation and how the sequence of events played out. This kind of event has had the power to make you feel incredibly bad about yourself. But after today it won't be so scary and disconcerting.

Now think about how that event may not have been so destructive, had it not tapped into the core belief that hovered beneath the surface. For instance, if the event involved a conflict, was the anger directed toward you more painful because it touched on a core belief that says you're unlovable?

Record everything you've remembered and learned about this event in your journal. Now write down any exceptions you recall to this negative core belief. If the belief is that you're unlovable, list experiences of being loved unconditionally, praised, or appreciated by someone. Remember what it felt like. Now write a summarizing affirmation statement based on experiences of being loved and valued. The next time someone is angry at you, think back to this statement as a new response to the Achilles heel.

_____

_____

_____

_____

_____

_____

_____

_____

_____

• • • • • • • DAY FOUR • • • • • • •
Challenging the Third Event

The Achilles heel is disarmed by affirmations because you're confronting an untrue, negative, self-harming thought with one that's truthful, positive, and self-loving. You have the power to focus on qualities in yourself that are unique and precious. We all have imperfections. Try to imagine that, at your core, you are perfect; that you have intrinsic worth, just as a newborn infant does. You may make mistakes, and struggle with some things more than others (better at math than in history), but these are your challenges. They are not who you are at your core.

Today, write down the third triggering event from your list. Identify the core belief that this event taps into. Then look at that core belief for a second after you've written it. Somewhere along the line you got the message that you weren't worthwhile in a fundamental way. It's a mistaken message—it's not who you are.

Now replace that flawed, negative core belief with some solid exceptions from your real life experience. Write about the qualities you possess that counter the old, negative beliefs. Then write an affirmation based on what you've learned. For example, "I'm a giver. I try to take care of the people I love. I don't have to be perfect to be worthwhile."

_____

_____

_____

_____

_____

_____

_____

_____

_____

_____

Challenging the Fourth Event

Today, write about your fourth triggering event. Remember the situation where this event occurred, and the negative core belief the event taps into. With the affirmation you create, you'll reframe the event as a challenge. Affirmations celebrate your strengths while allowing for imperfections. So, suppose you screwed up at work by missing a deadline. This triggers the core belief that you're incompetent. Fine—you missed a deadline. Does this have to mean that you're a total failure? Haven't there been plenty of times when you were on time, maybe even early?

Write your affirmation so that it allows for mistakes but also includes positive facts: "Even though I missed this deadline, I know that I have excelled numerous times" (describe ways you've excelled).

• • • • • • DAY SIX • • • • • •
Challenging the Fifth Triggering Event

By now you get the idea. Your Achilles heel really comes from a belief. The content of that belief is, on some level, that you are a bad, unworthy person. But just because you think that doesn't make it real. In fact, you have plenty of evidence in your life to show that it's not true. The good news is that the thought is only as powerful as you allow it to be. You can choose whether or not to buy into an old message that came from your parents, a teacher, or some other authority. You have the power to create a new thought, one based on a broader picture of reality. You can create a more balanced self-perception.

Today, write about your fifth Achilles-heel event. Describe when the event occurred and how you felt. What was the core belief it triggered? Recognize the belief as a mere thought. It's just a thought that pops into your head, penetrating your sense of self. You're going to replace that thought with another, and that thought is going to be the affirmation you use when you run into this kind of event again. Begin the affirmation with "My core belief is just a thought. I have the power to replace that thought with something more true." List positive evidence to counter your core belief:

_____

_____

_____

_____

_____

_____

_____

_____

_____

_____

_____

• • • • • • • DAY SEVEN • • • • • • •
Gathering Your Affirmations

Go back to the list of events you made on Day One of this week. Rewrite that list again today. But this time, after each type of experience that triggers your Achilles heel, write down the affirmation you've created to counter your core belief.

You will be creating a permanent reminder that this kind of experience is just that—an event that triggers a vulnerable place in you, making you feel insecure. However, every day this week you've gathered evidence that will help you climb out of the rabbit hole. When you feel overwhelmed in the moment, remember your affirmation and that you have strengths and positive qualities to balance this challenge.

The Worth Habit

Well done! It's week ten, and you've accomplished a lot. You've spent the past nine weeks honestly committed to rebuilding a healthy sense of self-esteem. This is no easy task. Although the critical voice in your head can seem completely reasonable and believable, the truth is that it just became a pattern, a strong habit you fell into. But you've learned throughout this journal that you can catch that voice in action and break the self-defeating pattern. You've learned to defend and uphold your right to feel and be worthy. You've put real work into making change happen, so take a moment to give yourself the credit you deserve.

Now you've got the skills to start a new habit—a habit of building and sustaining self-worth. If you keep working, eventually it will become natural, like a part of your hygiene routine—brush your teeth, comb your hair, notice something valuable about yourself!

Simply put, you're ready to allow in some self-love. It's time to bask in the glory of your strengths, skills, abilities, and positive attributes. Congratulations on learning to observe yourself without judgment as you move through work, schooling, love relationships, and friendships—every facet of your life.

This week, you're in the final phase, and all you have to do is to spend each day appreciating your worth. Notice when you:

- Put energy into pursuing your passions.

- Do well in your relationships.

- Use your curious, creative mind.

Each day this week, you'll gather evidence of your worth by noticing what you do right. You may not be used to appreciating yourself in this way, so it may feel weird at first. That's okay. The more you allow in good thoughts and reflections, the more natural it will feel.

Here are the rules to guide you this week:

- Search for evidence.

- Pay attention to the positive.

- Be willing to accept what's good in you.

Search for the evidence that you are a worthy person. Because you are. You just need to notice and accept the positive aspects of yourself. Pay attention to the moments that can open your eyes to who you truly are. Be willing to take off the blinders that keep you from letting in the good that is inherent in you.

This week, you'll focus on the ways you express your worth in six areas of life. Each day, you'll look for something positive in the ways you relate to others, how you express your personality, how other people appreciate you, your intelligence and creativity, the good you do in the world, and the ways you pursue what matters most to you in life.

You won't find something to celebrate in each of these domains every day, but if you look carefully, you'll notice several things a day worth appreciating.

From now on, you can record in your journal any evidence that supports your accurate, positive self-perception. As long as you are open to your worth, you can continue to develop it.

That's what this week is about—developing a habit of self-acceptance and a nonjudgmental view of yourself. Focus on your strengths. Appreciate your worth in every area of your life.

• • • • • • • DAY ONE • • • • • • •
Moving Past Negative Balancing

You have six domains of self-esteem from which to notice positive qualities in yourself. Again, although you may not find evidence in all the areas every day, surely you can appreciate positive qualities in one or several of the six areas. For example, perhaps today you'll notice one positive quality that represents how you relate to other people. What are your strengths in intimate relationships? What about with close friends, family, or coworkers? Are you warm, compassionate, or giving? Do you notice people anticipating this quality from you and appreciating it?

Write about the positive aspects you're able to notice, such as, "I make a real effort to be dependable." What does it mean to be dependable? Describe what this trait means to you: "I am reliable. When I commit to something, I keep my word and follow through on my obligation."

As you search for the positive qualities within the six domains, try to catch and counter any thoughts that negate the positive quality. Take note when your inner critic lobs a negative thought to contradict positive evidence of your worth. Write down in your journal what the inner critic said to you, then add specific, positive evidence that counters this negative point.

Finally, are you able to accept your worth as you reflect on these qualities? What does it feel like to stop and appreciate these strengths of yours?

_____

_____

_____

_____

_____

_____

• • • • • • • DAY TWO • • • • • • •
Going Blank

Today, begin by reviewing the six domains again and choosing a few to focus on. One thing that can happen as you search for positive qualities is the surreal experience of going blank. You look at the domains, and suddenly your mind cannot find one single shred of positive evidence. It's almost like you've forgotten who you are!

Reflect on your experiences, your history, and the choices you've made up to this point. No one else, not even a sibling, has seen and felt life exactly as you have. You have a set of emotions and behaviors that represent your unique experiences in this world.

Today, think about at least one quality that stands out and may even define you. For example, are you open and outgoing? Affectionate? A great mediator who helps people get along with each other? Spend a few moments reflecting on character traits that make you one of a kind.

First, define your unique and positive traits within the six domains. Now, what is one of your first memories of the trait or traits? How have they shown up in a situation recently? What did that feel like? Can you see how your positive traits have worth, and how you have strengths that make you different from others?

• • • • • • DAY THREE • • • • • • •
Being Your Own Best Friend

Today, you'll write about yourself from the perspective of someone who loves you and who you feel connected to. It's often easier for people who love us to appreciate who we are. They don't have the critical voice filtering out the positives; they can just value you for who you are.

Imagine how a best friend or lover would describe you. Think of what they'd say about your positive traits in several of the six domains of self-esteem. What do they appreciate about you? For instance, what would they say about your personality? Maybe you're outrageously funny, always seeing the weird and absurd in situations. Or they could talk about what a dependable friend you've been. How would someone who cares about you describe traits of yours?

Imagine how a loved one would complete this sentence, "I appreciate (your name) for being (trait/s) because (what positive impact you've had on them or others)." Still from this person's perspective, write about a way or time when this trait was helpful to them.

• • • • • • DAY FOUR • • • • • • •
The Big-Stuff-Only Problem

Sometimes we only take credit once we have reached some end goal—some great achievement or final hurdle. But the truth is you also need to focus on your mini-accomplishments. These are the small but significant ways you express yourself every day.

For instance, take your intelligence. You don't have to launch a rocket into space to show signs of intelligence. Your intelligence is marked by how you use your mind. It's seen in your ability to learn or understand or to deal with new situations; your ability to reason, analyze, or problem solve. It can also include your wisdom and insight. All you have to do is search for things you do or traits you possess, large or small, that are evidence of your intelligence. What are the skills you employ and in what area of your life?

For example, you may be good at problem solving, and your skills might be organization or creating systems. "I like to solve problems. Often, when problems come up at work between departments, I can see how we can devise a better system. I outline a plan for this alternative and share it with my coworkers. I feel proud of my ability to see how we can all do a better job with a more efficient system that benefits everyone."

Today, write about moments, decisions, or ideas you have that mark your mini-accomplishments in one or more of the six domains of self-esteem.

_____

_____

_____

_____

_____

_____

• • • • • • • DAY FIVE • • • • • • •
It's Not Boasting!

Next you'll record positive qualities about yourself while consciously acknowledging that you deserve to notice these things. It's quite possible that appreciating yourself feels uncomfortable to you. Perhaps it feels like boasting, and you were raised to be modest about your accomplishments. If this is the case, just remember that you're not suddenly going to transform overnight from having humility to becoming a braggart. The chances are slim that you'll become an obnoxiously proud person. Focusing on the positive qualities of your character is important, and it's something you've probably spent your whole life avoiding. Now it's time to shift your attention from that negative filter and let in some positive self-appreciation. Today, write about a quality that you possess in any of the six categories. Notice if you feel hesitant to blow your own horn because it feels like boasting. Allow that thought to enter your mind, but also allow it to pass. Don't hold onto it. We're giving you full permission to celebrate what's great about you.

For instance, if you choose to focus on a creative quality that you feel good about, describe the reason(s) you feel this quality deserves recognition. For example, "My best creative quality is my ability to prepare and cook interesting meals. I feel this quality deserves recognition because my family enjoys the nourishment I provide. I harvest vegetables from my garden and imagine new delicious dishes. I choose combinations of flavors and spices and imagine how they will taste." Allowing yourself to honestly acknowledge your positives can help you conquer the feeling-boastful syndrome!

_____

_____

_____

_____

_____

_____

• • • • • • • DAY SIX • • • • • • •
If a Tree Falls in the Woods

If no one witnesses your accomplishments or successes, is it hard for you to believe these achievements are valid? For instance, if you experience a moment privately in which you sense your worth, does it feel like it doesn't count because no one else acknowledged your feat? Society has ways of measuring our worth with grades, salaries, promotions, and so on. But this sends the erroneous message that you need these things to be worthy.

Today, remember past times and let these memories help you notice the moments *now* that reflect your worth. Take the time today to privately acknowledge what makes you worthy.

• • • • • • DAY SEVEN • • • • • • •
Final Reflections

Today you can conclude this journal with a sense of accomplishment. You've completed an important program for building self-esteem. Not only have you challenged negative thinking and replaced self-deprecating sentiments with worth-building messages, but you've also learned to gain a new perception of yourself based on your strengths, value, and intrinsic worth.

Every day this week you reflected on and wrote about the things you do right. This is a habit you can maintain over your lifetime. You have the tools to create a self-esteem journal with any blank notebook. Remember to search for the evidence of your strengths. Pay attention to positive and empowering moments in your life, and be willing to accept that you are worthy and valuable. Each day, look for the strengths and accomplishments in each of the six domains of self-esteem. You've got the skills to build self-esteem for the rest of your life!

Now go ahead and write about any improvement you've seen or felt in your self-esteem. How has it changed since the beginning of the program? Is it easier to recognize and focus on your worth rather than negative things about yourself?

From here on out, you have the tools for boosting your self-esteem. Although you may close this journal for now, at any time you can open a fresh journal and apply the exercises you've learned.

Matthew McKay, Ph.D., is a professor at the Wright Institute in Berkeley, CA. He is the author and coauthor of more than twenty-five books, including *The Relaxation and Stress Reduction Workbook, Thoughts and Feelings, Messages, When Anger Hurts, Self-Esteem* and *The Self-Esteem Guided Journal.* He received his Ph.D. in clinical psychology from the California School of Professional Psychology. In private practice, he specializes in the cognitive behavioral treatment of anxiety, anger, and depression.

Catharine Sutker is a freelance writer living in the San Francisco Bay Area. She is the coauthor of *The Self-Esteem Companion* and *The Self-Nourishment Companion.*

Also Available

SELF-ESTEEM
THIRD EDITION

MATTHEW MCKAY, PH.D.
PATRICK FANNING

With over 600,000 copies sold, this classic has long been the most comprehensive guide on the subject. Proven cognitive techniques help you talk back to the self-critical voice inside you and change the ways you think and feel about yourself.

ISBN 1-57224-198-5 / US $15.95

THE SELF-ESTEEM COMPANION

Simple Exercises to Help You Challenge Your Inner Critic & Celebrate Your Personal Strengths

MATTHEW MCKAY, PH.D.
PATRICK FANNING
CAROLE HONEYCHURCH, MA
CATHARINE SUTKER

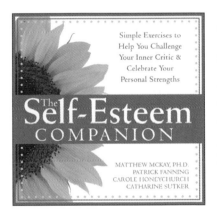

This motivating companion presents more than sixty simple exercises you can use to overcome a punishing inner critic. Make a realistic inventory of your abilities and weaknesses. Learn to celebrate your personal strengths. Each exercise includes tips for maximizing the technique's effectiveness and simple step-by-step instructions for putting it into practice.

ISBN 1-57224-411-9 • US $13.95
